SAME-SEX PARENTS

By
Holly Duhig

BookLife
PUBLISHING

©2018
BookLife Publishing
King's Lynn
Norfolk PE30 4LS

A catalogue record for this book is
available from the British Library.

ISBN: 978-1-78637-400-4

Written by:
Holly Duhig

Edited by:
Kirsty Holmes

Designed by:
Amy Li

All facts, statistics, web addresses
and URLs in this book were verified
as valid and accurate at time of
writing. No responsibility for any
changes to external websites or
references can be accepted by
either the author or publisher.

PHOTO CREDITS

Front Cover – Africa Studio, 2 – lazyllama, 4 – Monkey Business Images, DNF Style,
oneinchpunch, 5 – wavebreakmedia, Africa Studio, 6 – Rawpixel.com, 7 – Burlingham,
8 – tommaso lizzul, wavebreakmedia, 9 – CREATISA, 10 – Monkey Business Images ,
11 – Monkey Business Images , 12 – Olesia Bilkei, 13 – Africa Studio, 14 – FotoAndalucia,
15 – Oksana_Slepko, 16 – SpeedKingz, 17 – wavebreakmedia, 18 –Africa Studio,
19 – Gladskikh Tatiana, 20 – ristesju goce, wavebreakmedia, 21 – Rawpixel.com,
22 – Rawpixel.com, 23 – Monkey Business Images

Images are courtesy of Shutterstock.com.
With thanks to Getty Images, Thinkstock Photo and iStockphoto.

SAME-SEX PARENTS

Words that look like **this** can be found in the glossary on page 24.

Same-Sex Parents

There are many different types of family, and no two families are the same. Some children have one mum and one dad. Some children have two mums or two dads.

Having one mum and one dad is called having parents of the opposite **sex**. Having two mums or two dads is called having same-sex parents.

Opposite-Sex Parents

Same-Sex Parents

Why Do People Have Same-Sex Parents?

When someone has same-sex parents it's because two people fell in love and decided to start a family. Sometimes men fall in love with other men and women fall in love with other women.

When a man wants to be in a loving relationship with another man it is called being gay. When a woman wants to be in a loving relationship with another woman it is called being a lesbian. **7**

Making a Family

There are lots of ways of welcoming a baby into a family and lots of ways of becoming parents.

Some same-sex couples become parents by having their own children while others might **adopt** a child.

"A girl in my class asked me how my two dads could have made me. I told her that a nice lady called a **surrogate** helped them to make me so that they could start a family."

Penny – aged 7

What Is It Like Having Same-Sex Parents?

Having same-sex parents is no different to having opposite-sex parents. Same-sex parents take care of their children just like opposite-sex parents do.

Just like opposite-sex parents, same-sex parents take their children to the shops, to school and to the doctors when they are poorly.

People Might Ask Questions

Having same-sex parents is quite interesting. Because of this, people might ask you questions about your family. You don't have to answer any questions that you don't want to.

"My friend Sophie asked me who plaits my hair if I don't have a mum. I told her that my dads take it in turns to do my hair. Dads can plait hair too!"

Amber – aged 7

Sometimes people's questions can be rude. Sometimes people are rude by **accident**. Always tell a trusted adult if someone is rude to you on purpose.

"My friend, Louise, asked me which one of my two mums I call Dad. I said that neither of them are my dad. I call one of them Mum and one of them Mummy."

Alfie – aged 8

People Might Make Assumptions

Because having same-sex parents is interesting, people might make **assumptions**. This is when someone supposes something to be the case, without knowing. People might assume you have opposite-sex parents.

People make assumptions by accident.

"At school, we made cards for Mother's Day. I got to make two because I have two mummies!"

Simon – aged 6

These assumptions can make you feel like you are different. However, it's important to remember that lots of people have same-sex parents and that no two families are the same.

People Might Be Unkind

Most people are very **supportive** of same-sex families. They know that families come in all shapes and sizes. A small number of people might treat people from same-sex families unfairly. This is not OK.

All loving families are good. Remember, as long as you are happy, it doesn't matter what other people think.

"I love my mamas more than anything.

I wouldn't change my family for the whole world!"

Aisha – aged 6

There are some people who think that gay and lesbian couples shouldn't be allowed to form loving relationships and families. This is very unfair. These people might say hurtful things.

"My grandparents think my daddy and dad shouldn't get married. This makes me upset, but my parents say they should be able to marry whoever they fall in love with."

Rosa – aged 7

Treating someone unfairly because of who they love is a type of **discrimination** and is never OK. If someone says something hurtful to you, make sure you tell your parents or a teacher.

Celebrating Our Differences

We all have things that make us **unique**. You might have different hobbies and interests to your friends. For example, you might like sports while your friend likes painting.

What things make you unique?

All families are unique in some way or another. This is a good thing. Having same-sex parents is just one way in which your family can be unique.

Celebrating our differences can be fun!

Building a Community

It takes many different types of families to make a community. Treating everybody **equally** is the best way of building a community.

How many families make up your community?

What makes them all unique?

Families are very important. They help us grow and learn.
We should all feel **proud** of our families.

GLOSSARY

accident	without meaning to, or not on purpose
adopt	when a child joins a family legally, rather than through birth
assumptions	a thing that is accepted as true or as certain to happen, without proof
discrimination	treating someone unfairly for no good reason
equally	when everyone is treated with the same amount of respect
proud	feeling pleased and confident with something that is important to you
sex	either male or female
supportive	to provide support or show kindness
surrogate	a woman who carries a child for two people who want to be parents
unique	being the only one of its kind

INDEX

GREAT SCIENTISTS
CHARLES DARWIN

STEVE PARKER

Belitha Press

This edition published in 2002 by
Belitha Press
A member of **Chrysalis** Books plc
64 Brewery Road, London N7 9NT

Copyright © Belitha Press
Text © Steve Parker

Illustrations/photographs copyright © in this format
by Belitha Press

Typeset by Chambers Wallace, London
Printed in Malaysia

British Library Cataloguing in Publication Data
for this book is available from the British Library.

ISBN 1 84138 489 5

Acknowledgements

Photographic credits:
Bridgeman Art Library title page, 5, 12 top, 15 left,
    16, 21 top
Cambridge University Library this page
Bruce Coleman Limited 13, 14 top, 24 top
Edinburgh Photographic Library 6
E.T. Archive 20, 25
Mary Evans Picture Library 4 background, 7,
    10 top, 14 centre, 18, 21 bottom, 26
Robert Harding Picture Library 8, 11,
    12 bottom, 14 bottom, 15 right, 23
ICCE Photolibrary 27 left
Oxford Scientific Films Limited 24 bottom
Science Photo Library 10 bottom Dr Morley Read,
    27 right Lawrence Livermore Laboratory

Cover montage images supplied by Mary Evans
Picture Library and Ann Ronan Picture Library

Illustrations: Tony Smith 9, 19
Rodney Shackell 5, 8, 11, 17, 22

Editor: Kate Scarborough
Designer: Andrew Oliver
Picture researcher: Vanessa Kelly

Contents

Introduction

The theory of **evolution** is one of the most important ideas in the study of nature. It provides the basic framework for biologists who study living things. It helps us to put animals and plants into groups, and to work out the relationships between them. It guides our thoughts on why living things look and work as they do. It makes sense of **fossils**. And it is a vital part of the search for the origins of life itself.

Yet less than 150 years ago, the idea of evolution was almost unknown. Many scientists in the Western world believed the teachings of the Bible. These said that the different groups, or **species**, of animals and plants – from tigers to termites, trees to toadstools – had been created by God. The species were unchanged, the same now as they were on the day of creation.

A few scientists were toying with the idea that species might not always stay the same. They might change, or evolve, through time. But they could not explain how this happened.

Charles Darwin, a shy English **naturalist**, did. He proposed that there was a struggle for existence. Plants and animals produced more offspring than could survive. Nature itself chose, or selected, which animals and plants succeeded in the struggle to live, and which died. By this continuing process of natural selection (page 23), animals and plants gradually changed, or evolved, to survive better in their surroundings. Some species died out altogether, while new ones appeared.

Darwin's ideas caused a revolution in science and society. They have shaped the thinking of biologists and other scientists ever since.

Shrewsbury in Shropshire, England, in the mid 19th century. This mellow market town on the River Severn was Charles Darwin's home until he was about 16 years old, when he left for Edinburgh Medical School.

Chapter One
The Early Years

Charles Robert Darwin was born in Shrewsbury, England, on 12 February 1809. His father Robert was a doctor, and his mother Susannah was daughter of the famous potteries owner, Josiah Wedgwood. Charles' grandfather was Erasmus Darwin, well known in his time as a scientist with unusual ideas. He wrote on a range of subjects such as travel by air, exploring by submarine, and evolution.

Despite his learned father and eminent grandfather, Charles' early years were not outstanding. He attended Shrewsbury School, where the main lessons were in the classics, such as Latin. Many years later, he wrote: "I believe that I was considered by all my masters and by my father as a very ordinary boy, rather below the common intelligence."

Charles' grandfather Erasmus Darwin (1731-1802) wrote about scientific ideas in verse. His poem The Botanic Garden *described the classification system of the plant kingdom. In his work* Zoonomia *he put forward ideas about how the environment affects living things.*

Battle with a beetle

The young Darwin did find an interest of his own – collecting animals, plants, shells, rocks and other natural-history objects. He read *A Natural History of Selborne* by Gilbert White, which encouraged him to go out into the countryside, observing and collecting.

One day he pulled some old bark from a tree and found two rare types of beetle, so he grabbed one in each hand. Then a third rare beetle appeared. Not wanting to lose it, Darwin put it in his mouth. However the beetle's reaction was to squirt foul-tasting fluid, and he had to spit it out!

From medicine to religion

In 1825 Charles went to Edinburgh Medical School. He soon realized that medicine was not for him. He found the lectures dull, and he had to leave the operating theatre because he could not stand the horrors of surgery. (This was a few years before the first pain killer, chloroform, came into use.) So he gave up medicine, to the great disappointment of his father, who arranged the next-best career. In 1828 Darwin went to Cambridge University, to study the Bible and become a priest. Later, he wrote: "I did not then in the least doubt the strict and literal truth of every word in the Bible."

Planning an expedition

Despite being keener on shooting partridges than attending lectures, Darwin gained a Batchelor of Arts degree at Cambridge in 1831. He became friendly with two of the professors, geologist Adam Sedgwick and **botanist** John Henslow, and he continued to develop his interest in rocks, fossils, animals and plants.

Charles was supposed to study medicine in Edinburgh, from 1825 to 1827. But he spent much of the time furthering his boyhood interest in rocks, animals, plants and other aspects of nature.

Darwin then read *Personal Narrative* by the explorer Alexander von Humboldt. Rather than become a priest straight away, he decided to organize a natural-history expedition to the Canary Islands. By chance at the same time the Royal Navy was arranging a round-the-world **survey** expedition, under Captain Robert Fitzroy. Fitzroy asked Professor Henslow to recommend a naturalist for the expedition.

Henslow, knowing of Darwin's interest, recommended him for the job. At first Darwin's father refused to provide the money needed, but was eventually persuaded that this was an excellent opportunity for his son. On 27 December 1831, Charles Darwin set sail on the 235-ton **sloop-brig** HMS *Beagle*. The initial excitement was lost on Darwin, as he was seriously seasick!

Ideas on evolution

Charles Darwin was not the first to think of evolution. Many others had considered the subject. Their work helped him to form his ideas about *how* evolution happened.

● His grandfather, Erasmus Darwin, had vague ideas about evolution in his book *Zoonomia*.
● In the year Darwin was born, the French naturalist Jean-Baptiste Lamarck put forward the first scientific ideas on the subject, "transformation" as it was then called, in his book *Philosophie Zoologique*.
● Publisher and amateur geologist Robert Chambers wrote *Vestiges of the Natural History of Creation* in 1844, although Chambers did not admit he was author. It suggested the idea of evolution, and was condemned, mainly by the Church.

Alexander von Humboldt (1769-1859) was a famous German explorer and scientist who travelled to South America, North America and Asia. He was interested in many areas of science, from botany to astronomy (the study of planets and stars in space), and he wrote many popular books for non-scientific readers.

Chapter Two
Around the World on the Beagle

As the *Beagle* sailed across the Atlantic to South America, Darwin gradually recovered from his seasickness.

Arriving at San Salvador, Brazil, Darwin's eyes were opened to the wonders of nature. His tasks were to collect specimens of plants, animals, rocks and fossils, and to make surveys and notes at each place they visited. Soon the *Beagle* was crammed full of specimen cases, which were regularly shipped back to England.

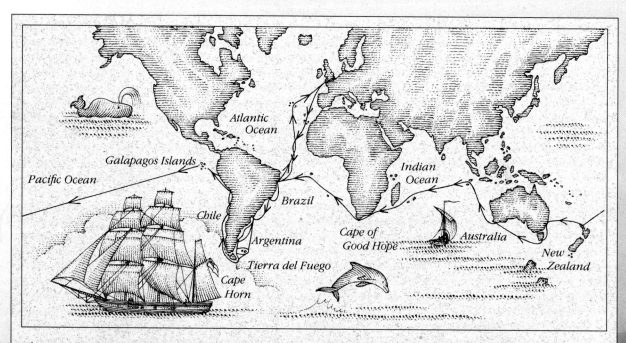

The Royal Navy commissioned Captain Robert Fitzroy (above) to make a round-the-world survey on HMS *Beagle*. They travelled to South America, rounded Cape Horn and headed up the coast to the Galapagos islands. Crossing the Pacific, the ship reached New Zealand and Australia. In each place, Darwin was busy collecting specimens from plant and animal life. From southern Australia, the *Beagle* crossed the Indian Ocean, went round the Cape of Good Hope back to Brazil and then home. The whole journey took five years, from 1831-1836.

The ten-gun Beagle *was about 27.5 metres (90 feet) long, weighed 235 tons, and had been launched in 1820. It had already made a long voyage to South America, and it then was overhauled and refitted for its five-year survey voyage with Fitzroy and Darwin.*

An early drawing of the bones of Megatherium. *This huge creature, 6 metres long, lived from a few million years ago to perhaps only several thousand years ago.*

Forests and fossils

Darwin was amazed by his first walks in a tropical rainforest, and wrote about "the general luxuriance of the vegetation . . . the elegance of the grasses, the novelty of the **parasitical** plants, the beauty of the flowers, the glossy green of the **foliage** . . ."

Nearby he found the huge fossilized head of an extinct giant sloth, *Megatherium*. Later in the voyage, at Port San Julian, Patagonia, he discovered fossils of another giant creature which seemed to be like a llama, but much larger.

Gradually questions began to form in his mind. Why had certain kinds of creatures died out, like the giant sloth and the huge llama? Ordinary sloths and llamas still lived in South America. There seemed to be some sort of relationship between the fossils and the living creatures.

The rainforest, where warmth and moisture combine to produce incredible abundance and variety in nature.

South American cattle men setting up camp for the night on the pampas. Darwin noticed that different grasses grew where cattle grazed.

Forces for change

As the *Beagle* sailed south, Darwin began to wonder about change in the natural world. In Argentina, he noticed that the coarse grass of the **pampas** no longer grew in the areas where cattle had been introduced. The new grass was smaller and finer. The cattle's grazing and droppings seemed to have changed the natural pampas grass, or allowed different grasses to flourish.

At the tip of South America, in Tierra del Fuego, Captain Fitzroy took ashore three Fuegian people he had seized on a previous voyage, as hostages for a stolen boat. Darwin marvelled at how the local people stood in the snow and sleet with only a few animal skins for protection. They slept on the wet ground, out in the open. He wrote: "Nature has fitted the Fuegian to the climate and productions of his miserable country." This was an early mention of how living things (in this case humans) change or adapt to their surroundings.

The record in the rocks

Charles Darwin collected many fossils on his voyage. At the time, fossils were known to be preserved remains of long-dead animals and plants. The accepted view was that they formed after a great catastrophe, such as Noah's flood, which killed most living things.

One awkward fact was that fossils from deep layers of rock were very unfamiliar, but those from shallower layers seemed more and more similar to the species of today. The great French fossil expert Baron Georges Cuvier explained this by saying there was a series of divine catastrophies. Each wiped out all forms of life. Then a new and improved selection of animals and plants was created to live on the Earth.

Continual change

In *The Principles of Geology* (1830-33), Charles Lyell wrote about the principle of uniformitarianism. This means simply that processes we see now in nature, such as coastlines being worn away by the sea, or earthquakes creating huge earth movements, happened in the past too. Over a very long time, they shaped the Earth we see today. This may seem obvious nowadays, but it was a new idea at the time.

Darwin read Lyell's book. He realized that changes in the living world, which he was observing on his travels, could also have taken place in the past. As the surroundings change, so might the animals and plants. Lyell's writings were very important as he began to form his ideas on evolution.

Earthquake in Chile

The *Beagle's* surveys followed layers of rocks along a 2,000-kilometre stretch of South American coast, from the Rio de la Plata to Tierra del Fuego. Darwin measured that the same rocks in the south were 100 metres higher above sea level than those in the north. The entire continent seemed to tilt. Had it moved since it was formed?

The ship rounded Cape Horn and sailed up South America's west coast. On 20 February 1835, a great earthquake shook the region. Entering the port of Concepcion, Chile, Darwin saw the appalling damage. He also noted that the rocks around the harbour had been lifted almost a metre by the earth movements. Shellfish and seaweeds which were normally near the water were now high and dry. Could such catastrophic changes in the surroundings be linked to changes in plants and animals?

An opossum from Argentina, one of the many animals Darwin described on his travels. American opossums are among the few types of marsupial (pouched) animals that live outside Australia.

Chapter Three
Evolution at the Equator

In 1835, the *Beagle* left South America and set sail across the Pacific Ocean. Almost 1,000 kilometres from the mainland, it anchored at a group of about 13 small, rocky islands on the Equator. They were the Galapagos Islands.

Darwin was at once struck by the strange nature of the birds, reptiles and other animals. He had never seen these particular species before – they seemed unique to the islands. Yet they had many similarities to species from the South American mainland.

Tortoises and finches

Stranger still, each island had its own kind of the animal in question. One example was the giant tortoises, weighing more than 200 kilograms, which the ship's crew rode like horses. The local people could tell which island a tortoise came from, by the shape of its shell.

There was also a different type of mockingbird on each island. Many of the flowers were unique to each island as well, yet similar to each other.

Giant tortoises lived on many Pacific islands besides the Galapagos. Today they are mostly very rare and protected by law.

Parts of the Galapagos are very rocky and jagged. The islands were formed by underwater volcanoes. Plant and animal life started on the islands about one million years ago.

Darwin was especially intrigued by one group of birds, the finches. They were mostly small and drab brown in colour. But each species had a slightly different size and shape of beak, which meant it could tackle a certain kind of food. Darwin wrote in his notebook: "One might really fancy that from an original **paucity** of birds in the **archipelago** one species had been taken and modified for different ends". The idea of evolution was taking root.

A marine iguana basking in the sun. These unique lizards dive into shallow water and eat seaweeds. This one comes from Hood Island.

A painting of a purple-stained orchid found on the Galapagos Islands. Again, Darwin found many varieties of orchid on the islands.

Darwin's finches

The 13 species of Galapagos finches live nowhere else in the world. Each species has a particular type of beak, which is suited to a certain kind of food. For example:

1. The large ground finch has a huge crushing beak for cracking tough seeds.
2. The medium ground finch has a slightly smaller but still strong beak, for cracking slightly smaller, hard seeds.
3. The warbler finch has a long, slim beak for probing into cracks and catching insects.
4. The small ground finch has a small but still strong beak, for cracking small, hard seeds.

Today, these finches are seen as a typical example of evolution. The Galapagos Islands formed from underwater volcanoes, only a few million years ago. It is thought that a few finches from South America landed there, blown by a storm. With other animals and plants already established, the finches had plenty of food. The original species evolved into many different species. Each adapted to a certain food source, so that they did not compete with each other.

The Maori people lived in New Zealand long before Europeans arrived. These canoeists in Milford Sound, South Island (left) are looking for food from the sea, such as fish and shellfish. The Maori person (below) was pictured in 1847, a few years after Darwin's visit. His feather-edged cape shows he is the chief of his group.

The Pacific coral islands

The *Beagle* sailed on across the Pacific to Tahiti, where Darwin fell in love with the misty peaks, tropical plants, colourful animals and the simple, natural lifestyle of the local people.

The journey continued on towards New Zealand and then Australia. He was shocked at the terrible living conditions of the local people. In their own lands, they were ruled over and made into slaves by the European settlers. This seemed to support his observations from the animal world, that the stronger always took over from the weaker.

In the Indian Ocean Darwin, now a seasoned traveller and still collecting specimens by the hundred, formed a theory of how coral barrier **reefs** and **atolls** were made (page 17).

Chapter Four
Back to England

The *Beagle* and its crew returned to Falmouth on 2 October 1836. Darwin spent the next few years organizing and cataloguing his vast collections of plants, animals, rocks and fossils. He was helped by Sir Richard Owen, who was later to become one of his main opponents (page 21).

In 1838 Darwin married his cousin Emma Wedgwood. The next year his book *Journal of Researches into the Natural History and Geology of the Countries Visited during the Voyage round the World of HMS Beagle* was a best-seller, despite its very long title. He had become a member of the Royal Society. In the same year, respected as a scientist and author, he moved to Down House near Bromley, in Kent, where he lived for the rest of his life.

The young Emma Wedgwood, who married Darwin. Among their ten children were the botanist Sir Francis Darwin and the mathematician Sir George Darwin.

Down House in Kent, home to Charles Darwin and his family for more than 40 years.

Coral creations

During Darwin's time, there were several ideas about how coral islands formed. One was that the circular coral atolls grew around the rim of a submerged volcano. Another was that the stony cup-shaped "skeletons" of the tiny coral animals grew and accumulated from the sea-bed upwards.

Darwin used his gifts for observation and sifting out the vital facts. He saw that corals grew only in the shallows, not in deep water. He reasoned that an undersea mountain, with its tip above the water, slowly sank or the sea level around it rose. The corals, trying to stay in the brightly-lit shallow water, built their stony skeletons one generation upon another. As the mountain sank, the rocky reef became thicker.

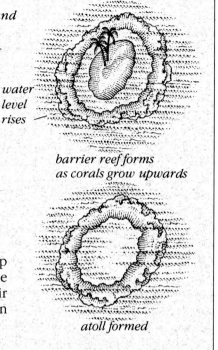

island

fringing coral reef

There are three stages in the formation of a coral atoll. Favourable conditions for its formation are shallow warm water, plenty of sunlight and nutrients.

water level rises

barrier reef forms as corals grow upwards

atoll formed

Work at Down House

During the 1840s and 1850s, Darwin continued his research and writing at Down House. For a time he returned to his first love, geology.

During the voyage of the *Beagle*, the coral lagoons of the Cocos Islands in the Indian Ocean had set him thinking about how these great limestone structures formed. His book *The Structure and Distribution of Coral Reefs* came out in 1842. Two years later he published *Geological Observations on Volcanic Islands*, and after another two years, *Geological Observations of South America*.

As time went on, his health began to fail. He could only do a few hours' work each day, and he took to walking in the gardens of his house and going on carriage rides. His illness was not identified, though it may have been a tropical sickness such as **Chagas' disease**, caught on his round-the-world voyage.

A flash of inspiration

Despite his ill health, Darwin continued his research into the idea of evolution. He was becoming more convinced that species were not fixed and **immutable**. They changed. He had written a short version of his ideas in 1842, but decided to collect every scrap of information he could, and to write a lengthy book with masses of evidence for his theory. He even talked to pigeon-keepers about the way they bred together selected birds, to produce new kinds of pigeon. This was a form of "**artificial** selection".

But *how* did species change in nature? What force made them alter gradually with time? One day while out in his carriage, Darwin came upon the idea of natural selection. It was like artificial selection, but nature did the choosing (page 23).

"Confessing a murder"

For many years, Darwin was reluctant to publish his ideas on evolution by natural selection. It meant that animals and plants evolved naturally. He now believed that God had not created them. However, most people at the time – including many scientists – still believed in the truth of the Bible.

In 1844 he wrote to his close friend Joseph Hooker, director of the Royal Botanic Gardens in Kew, London. He explained his worries: "I am almost convinced (quite contrary to the opinion I started with) that species are not (it is like confessing a murder) immutable". Like the Italian scientist Galileo two centuries before, Darwin knew that speaking out against the accepted teachings of the Bible was certain to offend and cause a storm of protest.

Darwin may never have finished this work on evolution, but for a letter which arrived at Down House in June, 1858, from Malaya.

Joseph Hooker (1817-1911) took over as director of Kew Gardens from his father, William. He travelled to India and the Himalayas (where he is in the picture below) and brought many plants back to England, including, in 1849, the now-familiar rhododendrons.

Malthus and the struggle for existence

Darwin was greatly influenced by a book called *An Essay on the Principle of Population* (1798) by Thomas Malthus, a clergyman, mathematician and economist. Malthus said that the human population could not keep going up for ever. Some day we would run out of food, living space and other things we need to live. Then there would be a "struggle for existence", and only the strongest and fittest would survive. He identified three "evils" which reduced our numbers – war, **famine** and disease. Darwin took Malthus' idea of "the survival of the fittest" and applied it to animals and plants in the natural world.

Charles Darwin at work in his study in Down House. In the late 1840s and 1850s he became very interested in the small seashore animals called barnacles, and he studied them in detail for eight years.

19

Chapter Five
The Book that Shook the World

The letter was from another English naturalist, Alfred Wallace. Wallace knew that Darwin was interested in evolution. So with his letter he sent his summary of the theory, titled *On the Tendency of Varieties to Depart Indefinitely from the Original Type*.

Darwin was amazed. All the work he had done so patiently for the past twenty years was neatly described by Wallace. He said: "Even his [Wallace's] terms stand as heads of my chapters".

Fellow scientists Lyell and Hooker advised that Darwin and Wallace should have their work read out as soon as possible to a scientific meeting. This happened at the Linnean Society in London, in July 1858. Then Wallace agreed that Darwin, who had gathered far more evidence to support their joint theory, should carry on with the idea, while he stood aside. Darwin did so, quickly finishing his great book. It was published on 24 November 1859 and called *The Origin of Species*.

Alfred Wallace

Alfred Wallace travelled widely in South America and the Far East, collecting specimens for museums. Like Darwin, he had been amazed by the fabulous variety of life in the tropical forests, and wondered how it came to be. While resting from a fever at his camp in South-East Asia, he remembered the same book by Malthus that Darwin knew. He had the same flash of inspiration, and came upon the idea of evolution by natural selection: "On the whole, the best fitted live. From the effects of disease the most healthy escaped; from enemies, the strongest, the swiftest, or the most cunning; from famine, the best hunters or those with the best **digestion**; and so on."

Alfred Wallace first worked as a surveyor for the new railways in England. At the age of 25 he began to travel and collect new kinds of animals and plants, deep in the jungles of South America and South-East Asia.

Charles Darwin and his new ideas became the subject of many jokes and comic pictures. As you can see from these cartoons, his theories were misunderstood. People thought that humans had evolved from living apes (not long-extinct ones), or even from living worms!

Reaction to The Origin of Species

The publisher of Darwin's book, John Murray, read it before printing, and realized a great outcry would follow. Only 1,250 copies were made. These sold out almost at once, so a second edition was produced.

People were indeed outraged. Darwin was denying the truth of the Bible! Scientists lined up to have their say. Former colleagues such as the famous naturalist Philip Gosse, Richard Owen (who had helped with the *Beagle* specimens), and Adam Sedgwick (the professor at Cambridge) turned against him. Louis Agassiz, professor at Harvard University and a follower of Cuvier, criticized him in North America. One clergyman called the quiet, mild-mannered Darwin "the most dangerous man in England".

But others rapidly recognized the good science in Darwin's ideas, and the vast amount of evidence which supported them. The biologist Thomas Huxley spoke for him in England, along with Hooker and Lyell. Professor of botany at Harvard University, Asa Gray, was his great supporter in North America. Darwin himself stayed at Down House and took little part in the arguments.

An ape for a father?

One misunderstanding about *The Origin of Species* concerned our own evolution. Popular newspapers and cartoons said that Darwin suggested humans had descended from living apes, such as gorillas or chimps. This was not true. His only mention of the subject was: "Much light will be thrown on the origin of man and his history."

There are only two kinds of elephants alive today, the African and Asian elephants. But fossils show that in the past, there have been many other members of the elephant group.

(1) Möenitherium: *a small animal that lived about 35 million years ago.*
(2) Trilophodon: *a long-jawed animal that lived in Africa, North America and Eurasia around 20 million years ago.*
(3) Platybelodon: *a shovel-tusked member of the elephant group that lived 10 million years ago. (4) The Imperial Mammoth: the largest of the elephant family with tusks like (5) the modern African elephant. The mammoth lived a million years ago. Evolution worked on the basic elephant design and fitted each kind to the conditions at the time. For example, the Imperial mammoth had very long, thick hair, to keep warm and survive the deep cold of the last Ice Age.*

Evolution by natural selection

Evolution simply means change. Animals and plants change with time. Darwin identified that nature did the choosing. The theory runs as follows:

Reproduction: parents have young which are like themselves, and different from other species. Tigers have baby tigers, lions have baby lions, and so on.

Too many young: not all the offspring can survive. Darwin calculated that in 750 years, one pair of elephants would have 19 million descendants – if they all survived.

Variation: not all the offspring are the same. There are slight differences in height, strength, colour, or other features. New variations crop up in each generation.

Natural selection: life is a struggle to find food, living space, mates, and other essentials. Some features might help in this struggle, such as sharper teeth in a hunter, or more seeds in a flower. These features make the individual better suited, or better adapted, to the surroundings. They improve its chances of surviving and breeding.

Inheritance: if a useful feature is **inherited**, the offspring of the animal or plant will have it too. It will help them to survive and leave even more offspring, who also possess the feature.

Evolution: over long periods of time, and many generations, features which improve survival become more common in a species. The species changes.

Origin of species: species which are better adapted to the environment gradually win. Those which cannot adapt die out. As the environment changes, species are always evolving and trying to stay well adapted.

What's in the Origin?

The Origin of Species by Means of Natural Selection, or the Preservation of Favoured Races in the Struggle for Life is a long but very readable book. It begins by looking at "variation under **domestication**", including pigeons, horses and garden flowers. Then it covers variation in nature, and the problems of identifying a species. It shows how the offspring of parents are all similar, but slightly different. These slight variations might give an individual a better chance of succeeding and staying alive. Chapters 6 and 7 deal with "difficulties of the theory, and objections", Chapter 8 with animal instincts, and the later chapters with fossils and the geographical ranges of species. Darwin draws evidence from all manner of animals and plants, from mice to elephants, asparagus to **furze bushes**. Yet he never explains the origin of any one particular species.

Domestication

Sheep were domesticated more than 10,000 years ago. They are needed for their wool, milk and meat. Above is an Australian domestic sheep, bred especially for wool and meat. Below is the barbary sheep bred for its milk and meat. Breeders use artificial selection to produce hundreds of varieties of sheep.

4

5

Chapter Six
The Struggle for Acceptance

The Origin of Species shocked and angered many people, including Darwin's own family. To accept the theory of evolution meant accepting that the account in the Bible, of the creation of animal and plant species, could not be true. Many scientists struggled to believe in both. Gradually, however, the theory of evolution by natural selection gained ground, and most scientists realized that Darwin was right.

Darwin did not retire after *The Origin of Species*. He kept up his studies and researches, and carried on with his experiments and nature observations in and around Down House. In 1871 he published *Descent of Man and Selection in Relation to Sex*. In this he concluded that humans are not the result of special creation, but they have evolved, like other animals. Their ancestors could be traced back far into prehistory. Ultimately, all living things are descended from the **"filament of life"** which his grandfather Erasmus had mentioned in his writings.

A stag's antlers and a peacock's tail are examples of sexual selection, a form of natural selection. Females choose the male with the most impressive features for their mate, and the male offspring inherit these features. Over a long time, male deer evolved bigger antlers to impress the female hinds. Peacocks with the finest tails were selected by the peahens.

Sexual selection

Natural selection says that the features of a living thing – its size, shape, colour, inner organs, body chemistry, behaviour, and so on – evolve to increase its chances of survival. But some features seem to reduce these chances. Surely the splendid, shimmering tail feathers of a peacock would get caught in the undergrowth, or be noticed by predators, and be a hindrance?

Darwin explained this by the process of sexual selection. Female peahens are attracted to and mate with the peacock with the most impressive tail feathers. This male will pass on the feature to his offspring. It is important to survive, but it is also vital to leave offspring.

Charles Darwin became very famous in his later years. He was visited by the foremost scientists, but he usually preferred to live a quiet life with his wife and family at Down House.

The final years

In the 1870s Darwin's health improved, and in 1877 he was awarded a special degree by Cambridge University. He continued to write books, about insect-eating plants, how plants grow and move, and how earthworms encourage decay and enrich the soil – they are "nature's first gardeners".

After a mild heart attack in December 1881, Darwin died peacefully at Down House on 19 April 1882, aged 73 years.

The storm of protest over *The Origin of Species* had died away. Charles Darwin had become a national figure and one of the best-known scientific names of all time. He was laid to rest at Westminster Abbey, London, next to the great Isaac Newton. The funeral was attended by dozens of politicians, inventors, explorers, scientists and artists, along with members of the scientific societies of many countries.

25

Chapter Seven
After Darwin

Darwin's work explained why animals and plants have the features they do. It made sense of the scheme for grouping and **classifying** species, devised mainly by the Swedish naturalist Carolus Linnaeus in the 18th century. Certain groups of species are similar because they are closely related, having evolved from the same ancestor.

It also explained fossils. They represented long-dead animals and plants, most of which had lost the struggle and become extinct. However some evolved into different species, which were successful for a while. Fossils traced these patterns of evolution through time.

Practical benefits

The theory of evolution by natural selection also had many practical results. It spurred research and field work, and gave scientists a basis on which to design their experiments and make observations. When looking at any feature of a plant or animal, the biologist asks: "What is it for? How does it help survival and reproduction?"

Mendel and inheritance

One problem, which Darwin always admitted, was that no one knew *how* features were passed on from parents to young. Why did offspring have some features of their parents, but not others? And why did offspring vary slightly?

At the time when *The Origin of Species* was causing such fuss, an Austrian monk was experimenting with peas in the peaceful monastery garden at Brno. His name was Gregor Mendel, and his work was the beginning of the modern science of **genetics**. It explained how certain features are inherited, controlled by what we now call **genes**. It showed how genes become shuffled and changed (mutated) from one generation to the next. Mendel's work was only recognized in about 1900. It solved many puzzles about inheritance, and filled some gaps in the theory of evolution.

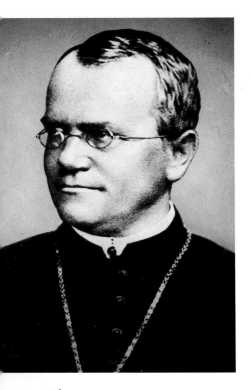

Gregor Mendel carried out many tests on peas. He observed how features such as the yellow or green colour, or smooth or wrinkled skin, were passed on from one generation of pea plants to the next, year after year.

Neo-Darwinism

In Darwin's day, the theory of evolution by natural selection became known as Darwinism. The more complete theory of evolution we have today is sometimes called neo-Darwinism (new Darwinism). It combines natural selection with the theory of heredity (see **inherit**) developed from Mendel's work, and with more recent developments such as the nature of mutation (change) and the discovery of **DNA**.

A false-colour image of a speck of DNA, the substance which passes on features from parent to offspring.

The Charles Darwin scientific research buildings on the Galapagos were named in memory of the island's most famous visitor. The islands are now part of Ecuador.

Evolution in fits and starts

Evolution generally takes a very long time. It happens over hundreds of generations, and thousands or millions of years. Many scientists assumed it was a gradual and continuing process.

In the 1970s, a newer idea said that evolution may often happen in fits and starts. Species stay the same for a very long time. Then they change rapidly in a burst of evolution, over a relatively short time, before settling down again. This theory is called punctuated equilibrium. It may be important in some groups of animals or plants, and it is still being discussed.

The World in Darwin's Time

	1800-1825	1826-1850
Science	**1801** Jean-Baptiste Lamarck publishes early ideas on evolution **1809** Charles Darwin is born **1825** George Stephenson's *Locomotion No. 1* begins the first regular steam railway service	**1842** Richard Owen invents the term "dinosaur" **1844** Robert Chambers is the unnamed author of *Vestiges of Creation* **1846** Planet Neptune is discovered
Exploration	**1820** Antarctica sighted for the first time, separately by a Russian, an American and an Englishman **1824** An exhibition of Aztec relics causes amazement in London	**1848** Henry Bates sets out for the Amazon, collecting around 14,000 species of insect in seven years
Politics	**1804** Napoleon becomes Emperor of France **1815** Duke of Wellington defeats Napoleon at Battle of Waterloo **1822** Brazilian Empire founded **1825** Indonesians rebel against Dutch in Java War	**1830** Belgium becomes an independent country **1837** Victoria crowned Queen of England **1842** "Opium War" in the Far East, Britain captures Hong Kong
Arts	**1817** Lord Byron writes *Darkness*, following the massive explosion of Tambora, Indonesia, that darkens the world's skies for a year **1823** Ludwig van Beethoven completes his Ninth Symphony	**1830** Eugene Delacroix paints *Liberty Leading the People* **1831** Katsushika Hokusai completes his series of landscape paintings *Thirty-Six Views of Mt Fuji* **1840** Houses of Parliament, London, designed and built by Charles Barry (completed 1865)

1859 *The Origin of Species* is published

1869 Dmitri Mendeleev produces the first periodic table of chemical elements

1876 Alexander Bell takes out a patent on his invention, the telephone

1879 Louis Pasteur makes discoveries that will lead to vaccination against many diseases

1882 Charles Darwin dies

1860 John Speke finds the source of the "White Nile"

1862 John Stuart succeeds on the first overland crossing of Australia

1871 Henry Stanley meets David Livingstone on the banks of Lake Tanganika, Africa

1879 Adolf Nordenskjold sails the North-East passage, along the Arctic coasts of Europe and Asia

1861 The various states of Italy come together as one country

1861 American Civil War begins

1867 Karl Marx publishes *Das Kapital*

1871 Germany becomes one country

1882 Politicians stop the building of the first Channel Tunnel between England and France

1897 Queen Victoria celebrates 60 years of rule

1851 Queen Victoria opens the Crystal Palace at London's Great Exhibition

1865 Jules Verne publishes *From the Earth to the Moon*

1874 First main exhibition of Impressionist paintings held in Paris

1879 Altamira prehistoric cave paintings, over 10,000 years old, discovered in Spain

1883 Robert Louis Stevenson writes *Treasure Island*

1894 The *Jungle Book* by Rudyard Kipling is published

Glossary

archipelago: a group of islands and even smaller islets.

artificial: not natural, but man-made. In artificial selection, people select the animals they wish to breed together, to produce new varieties. In natural selection, nature does the choosing.

atoll: a low, ring-shaped island or group of islands in the ocean. The area of water in the middle is called a lagoon.

botanist: a person who studies plants, from seaweeds and mosses to flowers and trees.

Chagas' disease: an illness from the tropical regions of South America. It is caused by a microscopic animal that multiplies in the body, and it is spread in the droppings of certain insects. A similar animal causes sleeping sickness in Africa.

classify: to put things into groups, which are then put into larger groups, and so on. All furry, warm-blooded animals are classified as mammals.

digestion: when food is cut up, chewed and broken down into a soup of tiny pieces, ready to be absorbed into the body.

DNA: deoxyribonucleic acid, a chemical which forms the *genes* that are passed on from parents to young.

domestication: the process by which a group of wild animals are made tame and useful to humans – on the farm, when hunting, or as pets (see *artificial*). People have domesticated sheep, goats, cattle, oxen, horses, dogs, cats, goldfish and many other creatures.

evolution: change with time, especially in animals and plants.

famine: large-scale starvation, when many people become ill and die due to lack of food.

filament of life: a popular name for the first kinds of life, like shapeless microscopic threads, to appear on Earth.

foliage: a word for the leaves on trees and bushes.

fossils: the bones, teeth, shells, bark and other long-dead remains of once-living things, which have turned to stone and are preserved in the rocks.

furze bushes: another name for prickly gorse bushes, which have green spiky leaves and yellow flowers.

genes: the microscopic bits of chemicals (see *DNA*) that carry information, in a form of code, which tell an animal or plant how to grow and live.

genetics: the scientific study of how features are passed from parents to offspring, and also how they change. In people, these features include eye and skin and hair colour. See also *inherit*.

immutable: fixed, and unable to change.

inherit: when features such as eye or hair colour are passed on, or inherited, from parents to young (see *genes*).

naturalist: a person who studies animals, plants, rocks and other aspects of nature.

pampas: the rolling grasslands of South America (similar to the prairies in North America, savannas in Africa, and steppes in Asia).

parasitical: when a living thing is a parasite and "steals" nourishment from another, such as a flea that sucks blood, or a plant parasite like mistletoe.

paucity: a poorness or lack, as opposed to an abundance.

reef: jagged rocks at or just below the water's surface. They have usually been built up over thousands of years from the stony cup-shaped skeletons of millions of tiny, anemone-like coral animals.

sloop-brig: a type of sailing ship with three masts and square-shaped sails.

species: a group of animals or plants that have been *classified* together. Members of one species can breed with each other, but not with members of another species.

survey: when an area is studied and mapped to show the hills, valleys, coasts, water and islands, and the kinds of soils and rocks on the surface, and the plants and animals living there.

Index

Agassiz, Louis 21
Argentina 8
Australia 8, 15

barnacles 19
HMS *Beagle*, voyage of 7-16
Bible, the 4, 6, 18, 21
Brazil 8

Cambridge University 6, 25
Chagas' disease 17, 30
Chambers, Robert 7
Chile 12
Cocos Islands 17
coral islands, formation of 15, 17
Cuvier, Georges 11, 21

Darwin, Charles (1809-1882)
    education 5-7
    funeral 25
    home life 5, 16-19, 24, 25
    ill health 17, 25
    in Pacific/Indian oceans 15
    in South America 10-12
    later work 24, 25
    on the Galapagos Islands 13, 14
    theory of evolution 18-23
Darwin, Erasmus 5, 7, 24
DNA 27, 30
domestication 23, 30
Down House 16, 18, 21, 24, 25

earthworms 25
Edinburgh Medical School 6
elephant, evolution of 22, 23
*An Essay on the Principle of
    Population* (T. Malthus) (1798) 19
evolution, theory of
    after Darwin 26, 27
    before Darwin 7
    Darwin's observations of evolution
        in nature 8-15
    Darwin's theory of evolution 12,
        18, 22, 23
    Lyell's contribution 12, 20 21
    Malthus' contribution 19, 20
    Wallace's contribution 19, 20
    what evolution is 4, 22, 27

finches of Galapagos 14
Fitzroy, Robert 7, 8, 11
fossils 4, 10, 11, 22, 26, 30

Galapagos Islands 13, 14, 27
genes 26, 30

genetics 26, 30
*Geological Observations on Volcanic
    Islands* (C. Darwin) (1844) 17
*Geological Observations of South
    America* (C. Darwin) (1846) 17
geology 6, 12, 16, 17
Gosse, Philip 21
Gray, Asa 21

Henslow, John 6, 7
heredity, theory of 27
Hooker, Joseph 18, 20, 21
von Humboldt, Alexander 7
Huxley, Thomas 21

inheritance, principle of 22, 24,
    26, 30

*Journal of Researches into the
    Natural History and Geology of
    the Countries Visited during the
    Voyage round the World of HMS
    Beagle* (C. Darwin) (1839) 16

Lamarck, Jean-Baptiste 7
Linnaeus, Carolus 26
Linnean Society Meeting (1858) 20
Lyell, Charles 12, 20, 21

Malthus, Thomas 19, 20
Mammoth, Imperial 22
Maoris 15
Megatherium (sloth) 10
Mendel, Gregor 26, 27
Möenitherium (elephant
    ancestor) 22

A Natural History of Selbourne
    (G. White) (1789) 5
neo-Darwinism 27
New Zealand 15

The Origin of Species (C. Darwin)
    (1859) 20-26
Owen, Richard 16, 21

pampas 11, 30
Personal Narrative (A. von
    Humboldt) 7
Philosophie Zoologique (J-B.
    Lamarck) 7
Platybelodon (elephant ancestor) 22
The Principles of Geology (C. Lyell)
    (1830-33) 12
punctuated equilibrium 27

religion 4, 6, 18, 21

Sedgwick, Adam 6, 21
selection
    artificial 18, 23, 30
    natural 18, 22-24, 26, 27, 30
    sexual 24
Shrewsbury 4, 5
species
    change in 4, 11, 13, 14, 18, 26
    classification of 10, 22, 26
'survival of the fittest' 19

Tahiti 15
*The Descent of Man and Selection
    in Relationship to Sex* (C. Darwin)
    (1871) 24
The Origin of Species (C. Darwin)
    (1859) 20-26
*The Structure and Distribution of
    Coral Reefs* (C. Darwin) (1842) 17
Tierra del Fuego 11, 12
tortoises, giant 13
Trilophodon (elephant ancestor) 22

uniformitarianism 12

*Vestiges of the Natural History of
    Creation* (R. Chambers) (1844) 7

Wallace, Alfred 20
Wedgwood, Emma 16, 25
Wedgwood, Josiah 5
White, Gilbert 5

Zoonomia (E. Darwin) 7